# Is That a
# Skunk?

Gary Bogue &ast; Illustrated by Chuck Todd

Heyday, Berkeley, California

Library of Congress Cataloging-in-Publication Data

Names: Bogue, Gary, author. | Todd, Chuck, illustrator.
Title: Is that a skunk / Gary Bogue ; Illustrated by Chuck Todd.
Description: Berkeley, California : Heyday, [2018] | Audience: Ages 4-8. |
  Includes bibliographical references.
Identifiers: LCCN 2016056956 | ISBN 9781597143998 (hardcover : alk. paper)
Subjects: LCSH: Skunks--Juvenile literature. | Animal behavior--Juvenile
  literature.
Classification: LCC QL737.C248 B64 2018 | DDC 599.76/8--dc23
LC record available at https://lccn.loc.gov/2016056956

Book Editor: Molly Woodward
Interior Design: Rebecca LeGates
Cover Design: Diane Lee

Orders, inquiries, and correspondence should be addressed to:

Heyday
P.O. Box 9145, Berkeley, CA 94709
(510) 549-3564, Fax (510) 549-1889
www.heydaybooks.com

Printed in China by Regent Publishing Services, Hong Kong

10 9 8 7 6 5 4 3 2 1

This is for the striped skunk family that lives in MY backyard. —Gary Bogue

To the Chen Family—Wei, Eileen, Landon, and Kylie—for their generous help portraying the family in our backyard skunk adventure. —Chuck Todd

One morning, Lucas and his family are having breakfast when Lucas spots something. "Is that a skunk?" he says.

"Where's Hotdog?" Mom shouts. "Make sure he doesn't get outside with that thing."

They wait for the skunk to leave the
doghouse. But the skunk doesn't leave.

Now what?

Days pass.

Lucas, Ellie, and Hotdog
have fun taking afternoon walks.

So does the skunk!

One day, Lucas and Dad meet the skunk outside their front door.

"YIPES," Dad whispers. "Back away slowly."

Luckily, they make it inside unsprayed.

"This skunk has us surrounded," Lucas says.
"Why is it hanging around our yard?"
He decides to do some research.

GOOGLE: Where do skunks live in town?

They live under houses. Under decks. They crawl
in by tearing off vent screens. Sometimes they live
under piles of wood and debris in backyards.

AND...sometimes they live in doghouses.

GOOGLE: What do skunks usually eat in someone's backyard?

They hunt for snails, mice, earthworms, lizards, snakes, grasshoppers, crickets, berries, and fruit that falls from trees.

Lucas's family begins to get used to the skunk living in their backyard. They even begin to like the skunk. It has become a neighbor of sorts—a neighbor they don't want to go near.

But one afternoon, Lucas can't find Hotdog.

And then everyone hears barking.
They run outside. Oh no!

**Too bad Hotdog didn't know these warning signs:**

Skunk staring at you means:
"Don't do anything to scare
me, or else."

Skunk stamping its front
paws means: "Go away
or I will spray."

The worst thing you can do is bark and run after a skunk. Too late.

Poor Hotdog.

Skunk lifting up its tail means: "Last chance."

Skunk doing handstand (pawstand?) means: "Too late! Get ready!"

And then the stink hits them.

Hotdog runs in circles, rolls around on the grass, even turns somersaults trying to rub off the horrible stench.

Lucas knows it's probably no use.

Then he notices something in the doghouse.
And everything begins to make sense.

Hotdog needs a bath. Mom mixes up a special cleaning formula from a pet column she found in their local newspaper.

# Make Skunk Smell Go Away

Mix 1 quart of 3 percent hydrogen peroxide, 1/4 cup of baking soda, and 1 teaspoon of liquid soap (like Dawn).

Use the mixture to wash your sprayed pet. Be sure to keep it out of your pet's eyes, nose, and mouth. Rinse with tap water. This amount of the mixture works for small dogs. Double it for medium dogs. Triple it for big dogs.

Everyone helps wash Hotdog while the skunk family watches from the doghouse.

Lucas finds out that the babies will need to live in the doghouse for another month. It is easy to let them stay.

Early one evening a few weeks later, someone leaves the kitchen door open and Hotdog slips out into the backyard. He is curious but doesn't bark. He and Mama skunk just stare at each other as the skunks walk away from the doghouse.

It is time for the teenage skunks to start learning how to live on their own.

Lucas and his family watch from the window as the skunk family heads for a hole under the fence.

The skunks are off to see the world, and Hotdog has reclaimed HIS doghouse.

# Skunks

A Report by Lucas

There are four kinds of skunks in North America: striped skunks, spotted skunks, hognose skunks, and hooded skunks.

striped

spotted

hooded

hognose

Skunks usually get along with cats and opossums.

Skunks don't usually get along with dogs.

Skunks have to watch out for:

**Owls.** Great horned owls can't smell skunks'
stinky spray, so they have no problem catching
skunks and eating them.

**Cars.** Cars can't smell skunks' stinky spray,
either. They hit and kill lots of skunks.

Don't leave food for cats and dogs outside. Skunks, opossums, and raccoons find and eat it at night. It makes them come back to your yard.

Put seed catchers under your bird feeders to catch falling birdseed. Skunks like to eat birdseed they find on the ground.

**Signs of skunks digging in your yard:** They leave little trenches about three inches wide by five inches long as they search for earthworms and grubs.

**Skunk spraying power:** Skunks can spray to distances of fifteen feet. The odor is so potent it can be smelled more than a half mile away.

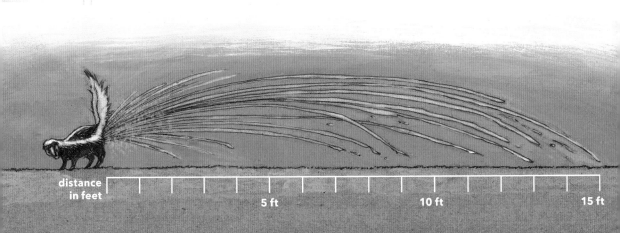

distance in feet

5 ft          10 ft          15 ft

# More about Skunks

## Websites

Learn skunk facts: animals.nationalgeographic.com
  /animals/mammals/skunk

Watch skunk videos: www.arkive.org/striped-skunk
  /mephitis-mephitis

Find out how to manage skunks humanely:
UC Integrated Pest Management: http://www.ipm
  .ucdavis.edu/PMG/PESTNOTES/pn74118.html
Havahart: http://www.havahart.com/skunk-facts


## Books

Bodden, Valerie. *Skunks*. Mankato, MN: The
  Creative Company, 2016. (ISBN: 9781628322200)

Mason, Adrienne and Nancy Gray Ogle. *Skunks.*
  Toronto, Canada: Kids Can Press, 2006.
  (ISBN: 9781553377344)

Swanson, Diane. *Welcome to the World of Skunks.*
  Vancouver, Canada: Whitecap Books, 2010.
  (ISBN: 9781551108551)

**Gary Bogue** was curator of the Lindsay Wildlife Museum in Walnut Creek, California, for twelve years. He also wrote a daily column about pets and wildlife for the *Contra Costa Times* and Bay Area News Group for forty-two years, and authored *There's an Opossum in My Backyard, There's a Hummingbird in My Backyard,* and *The Raccoon Next Door.*

**Chuck Todd** is an award-winning illustrator and visual journalist in the San Francisco Bay Area. After more than two decades as a newspaper artist and presentation editor, Chuck has turned his focus to creating illustrations for children's books, magazines, websites, and comics. This is his fourth illustrated wildlife book with author Gary Bogue. See more of Chuck's illustration work at www.chucktodd.net.